POWWOW

Pheasant plumes make up the headdresses of the Tlacopan Aztec dancers from Mexico City.

POWWOW

A GOOD DAY TO DANCE

WRITTEN AND PHOTOGRAPHED BY
JACQUELINE DEMBAR GREENE

A First Book

FRANKLIN WATTS • A DIVISION OF GROLIER PUBLISHING
NEW YORK   LONDON   HONG KONG   SYDNEY   DANBURY, CONNECTICUT

For Joel "Little Man" Gauthier and his family, with thanks for extending the hand of friendship in the true spirit of powwow.

—J. D. G.

Note to readers: Definitions for **bold** terms in the text can be found at the end of this book.

Subject Consultant
Dr. Frederick J. Dockstader

Photographs ©: Jacqueline Dembar Greene

Visit Franklin Watts on the Internet at:
   http://publishing.grolier.com

Library of Congress Cataloging-in-Publication Data

Greene, Jacqueline Dembar.
   Powwow : a good day to dance / written and photographed by Jacqueline Dembar Greene.
      p. cm. — (A first book)
   Includes bibliographical references and index.
   Summary: Follows the activities of a young boy as his family attends a Wampanoag powwow, describing the significance of some of the events at the gathering, particularly the dances.
   ISBN 0-531-20337-9 (lib. bdg.)   0-531-15926-4 (pbk.)
   1. Powwows—Juvenile literature. 2. Wampanoag Indians—Juvenile literature. [1. Powwows. 2. Indian dance—New England. 3. Wampanoag Indians. 4. Indians of North America—New England.] I. Title. II. Series.
E98.P86G74 1998
394—dc21   97-32392
                                                                CIP
                                                                AC

CONTENTS

Feathers on the regalia of a young Fancy Dancer seem to fly as he turns.

INTRODUCTION
POWWOWS OLD AND NEW

IN THE ALGONQUIAN LANGUAGE, *pauwau* was the name given to a medicine man and also referred to a ceremony that he performed. Europeans mispronounced the word as *powwow* and used it to refer to any large gathering of Native Americans.

For hundreds of years, small bands of Indians came together in large tribal villages at different times of the year to visit, exchange news, and entertain each other with stories. People shared meals, gave gifts of food and clothing, and danced. Most gatherings were of just one tribe, but some were held to renew friendships with other tribes. Today, powwows have become a chance for Native Americans to preserve their traditions and celebrate their culture.

At all powwows, the people dance. Dancers move to the rhythm of the drum, which is the heartbeat of the powwow, and tap their feet to honor Mother Earth. In the early days, each dance was a personal prayer. People danced to "make medicine"—that is, to ask the Creator to help during a time of trouble, or to cure a sick friend or relative. Some dances honored the warriors who protected the people, or the women who brought forth the gift of new life. Sometimes dances imitated an event or animal of special importance. There were Rain Dances, Buffalo Dances, Deer Hunt Dances, and Eagle Dances.

At traditional powwows, men and women sat in circles and discussed issues. Slow Turtle, former Supreme Medicine Man of the Wampanoag Nation, said that when the pilgrims landed, members of the tribe probably gathered to discuss how to deal with the newcomers. Today, most issues are discussed in tribal council meetings, but powwows still present opportunities for Native Americans to talk about ideas and problems relating to their tribes.

Today's powwows are intertribal, bringing together many different Native American nations. Men, women, and children all dance, and clothing and dance styles reflect many tribes. Non-Indian visitors are often welcome to attend and share the culture and spirit of the gathering. Dance contests for all ages add excitement. The tradition of gift giving continues, with friends sharing food and handmade items. Elders see traditions passed down, as old stories are heard by young ears. Children learn traditional dances and make and wear clothing that reflects their heritage. Time spent at a powwow is filled with activity as people discover that powwow days are a good time to dance.

A group of young
boys waits to dance.

~1~

GRAND ENTRY

THE MEDICINE MAN walks slowly around the dance circle. The ribbons on his shirt ripple in the breeze. In his right hand, he carries an abalone shell filled with smoldering herbs. With his left hand, he uses a large turkey-feather fan to send the smoke toward the crowd as a blessing. The sweet scent of burning sage drifts through the air. Ten-year-old Little Man stands quietly and breathes in the fragrant smoke. Soon he will join the dancing. The powwow is about to begin.

Little Man has seen many opening ceremonies, and each is a little different. An open field is the setting of this gathering. A large dance circle is roped off in the center. Dancers and their families sit on

A medicine man uses a feather fan to send smoke from burning sage as a blessing to the crowd.

hay bales and stools inside and outside the circle. They are all waiting to dance. Spectators sit on chairs and blankets, waiting for the powwow to begin. A tribal leader steps to the front of the arbor covered with green pine boughs, where the singers sit around their big drum.

The announcer's voice booms out across the crowd: "We call upon our modern warriors, the Native American veterans, to lead the procession into the circle."

Everyone stands, and people take off their hats out of respect for the men and women who have

A drum group sings under a shaded arbor inside the dance circle.

fought in American wars. A color guard carries the American flag, and an honored leader holds the tall wooden staff that represents the Native American Nation. Eagle feathers flutter atop the staff as he lifts it proudly. Little Man watches the procession. Some veterans wear army uniforms decorated with military medals and traditional Native American items, such as eagle feathers and **medicine wheels**. He wonders what deeds or acts of bravery each has performed to earn the sacred eagle feathers.

The drum begins a slow, steady pulse. Little Man feels the drumbeat moving up through the earth, tickling his moccasined feet, telling his legs to move with the rhythm. He is ready to dance, but he has to wait. The announcer speaks again: "We invite all veterans and their families to join the procession." Many people standing outside the circle or seated in the stands step forward as the procession snakes around the dance circle.

It's almost time, Little Man thinks. He sways to the deep, echoing pulse of the drum. He is wearing his finest traditional clothes, called **regalia**. The stiff porcupine hairs on his headpiece, called a **roach**, rustle together. A small medicine wheel dangles from a lock of his hair.

Little Man's friend, Moose, joins him. "It's warm today, but not too hot," Little Man says to him. "A good day to dance."

"I don't care if it's sunny or cloudy or windy," Moose replies. "If we're at a powwow, it's always a good day to dance."

Little Man nods. "A good day to dance, and eat **fry bread**."

"You're making me hungry," Moose says, "and it's still morning!"

The smoke from the burning sage has drifted away, and as Little Man sniffs the air, he smells food cooking at the stalls around the edge of the

13

WAMPANOAG TRIBE

Historically, the Wampanoag tribe occupied lands in what is today Massachusetts and the eastern portion of Rhode Island. Today, the two main branches of the tribe are the Mashpee Wampanoags of Cape Cod, and the Gay Head Wampanoags of Martha's Vineyard.

When colonists from England arrived in the 1600s, members of the tribe taught the newcomers farming and hunting techniques and gave them food and assistance to survive. As more settlers arrived, the tribe was pushed into smaller territories. At various times, the Wampanoags were given control of their own government on established lands. By the mid-1800s, they had lost much land, and the tribe struggled to maintain its independence.

A strong movement for preserving Wampanoag culture and history developed in the early 1900s. At that time, the ancient tradition of holding large tribal gatherings was renewed, and members of many Indian nations were invited. The Mashpee Wampanoags of Cape Cod have held a powwow on the first weekend of July every year since 1924. Today, non-Indian visitors are welcome to watch the traditional dancing, hear stories, feast at a clambake, and watch the nighttime fireball game.

Little Man and an Oneida friend, Jonathan, sample fry bread.

campground. He smells the thick dough called fry bread frying on griddles. He can almost taste a hot mouthful sprinkled with sugar. The breeze carries the smell of buffalo burgers sizzling over coals, and buffalo stew and venison simmering in huge pots. At this Wampanoag gathering in Mashpee, Massachusetts, many booths also serve thick quahog chowder and crispy clam cakes, made from fresh Atlantic Ocean clams.

Little Man remembers the powwow in the spring when he met Moose and his family. It was a three-day powwow held over the Memorial Day weekend. As he and Moose talked, they discovered they were both the same age, and they both loved dancing. They made lots of trips to the food booths that weekend, too!

Moose's war-dance regalia includes a headpiece, breastplate, vest, and feather bustle.

-2-
DANCING
TO THE
DRUM

ALL THE DANCERS check their outfits to make sure that everything is fastened tightly. If any item drops into the circle, a dancer will be disqualified from competition. If an eagle feather falls to the ground, all dancing stops and a special ceremony is held before it is returned to its owner.

Moose is dressed in his full wardance regalia. He adjusts his headpiece. The porcupine hairs bristling on his head roach are dyed red. Over his ribboned shirt, he wears a **breastplate** that his father made out of dozens of deer bones, called **hairpipe tubes**. Small beads are strung between them.

17

His buckskin **breechcloth** and black vest are embroidered with brightly colored beads. His mother has spent weeks sewing the colorful designs. On his back, Moose wears a large **feather bustle**, a treasured addition to his dance outfit. The swaying bustle is filled with a thick circle of eagle feathers. Moose's parents bought his first dance bustle from a Native American craftsman and gave it to him as a gift. The new one he wears was made for him by his father.

Moose's sister, Cassie, runs up and joins the boys outside the dance circle. Clanking and tinkling sounds fill the air.

"You sure can't sneak up on anybody," Moose teases her. "We heard you coming a mile away with all those jingles." Cassie is a **Jingle Dress** dancer. Rows and rows of tin cones formed out of tobacco can lids hang from her cloth dress. They clink and tinkle as they move against each other. In the early days of jingle dress dancing, women rolled the flat tin lids into cones. Now, the cones can be purchased and attached with pliers onto strips of cloth hanging in rows on the dress. When Cassie dances, her graceful stepping and swaying makes the shiny metal cones sing in rhythm with the beating drum.

Dancing is the highlight of powwows. Little Man had watched the dancing when he was

Rows of tin cones hang from the cloth of a jingle dress. ➤

younger. Soon he learned to recognize the different styles and decided which dance he especially wanted to learn. He imitated the dancers he admired, and a family friend showed him some steps.

There are three main types of dances for men and boys. The war dances were originally danced before a battle to ask the Creator for success and bravery. Some were danced after a raid to show other members of a village what had happened. Now, **Men's Traditional** is a slow war dance. **Fancy Dance** is a fast war dance with elaborate regalia and quick, athletic movements. **Grass Dance** is not a war dance at all. The men usually don't wear feathers or other traditional dance items, such as bustles. Instead, they wear outfits fringed with long colored yarns or ribbons, which sway with their dance movements like tall prairie grass rippling in the wind. They dance on one foot, and then the other, leaning into their steps as if they are about to lose their balance. Some elders say this dance originated among the Plains Indians, whose men danced for hours before every gathering, so that the long, rough grasses within the circle would be flattened for the rest of the dancers.

Women and girls also dance in one of three main categories. In addition to Jingle Dress, there is **Women's Traditional Dance.** Dancers circle the ring in a stately movement. They keep their heads

A traditional dancer concentrates during a competition event (top).

A grass dancer tilts and sways like prairie grass (bottom).

Fancy Shawl dancers compete with fast, high steps.

and backs straight while their feet step slowly to the steady beat, beat, beat of the drum. The fringes on their dresses and shawls swing in time to the sound. In **Fancy Shawl Dance**, the women open their bright, long-fringed shawls and swirl with a fast, high step. Their shawls are a newer variation of the blankets women used to wrap around their shoulders.

At most modern powwow gatherings, there are competitions with prizes in every category. At some powwows, dancers compete for large awards of money. At a powwow in Virginia, Little Man won a first prize. He dances in the Boys' Division, for boys ages six to eleven. He is often chosen among the best dancers. Moose has won so many competitions that he moved to the Junior Boys category, for young men between the ages of twelve and seventeen. It is exciting for him to challenge his dance skills with stiff competition. Although he is younger than all the other dancers in this category, he still wins many prizes.

"Okay, all you young dancers!" calls the announcer. "Come into the circle of life! Come into the dance circle!" Boys and girls of all ages join the intertribal procession as the dancers do a slow, traditional step. Little Man enters with the line of dancers through an opening on the eastern side. The dancers move in a clockwise direction, filling the circle from the edges to the center.

Little Man looks around at the colorful face paint some people are wearing. The flowing fringes on dresses, shawls, shirts, and grass-dance regalia seem to fly on the breeze. Feather bustles sway, animal headpieces bob, and the air is filled with the sounds of clinking leg bells, clacking **deer toe** rattles, and tinkling jingles.

Little Man feels the excitement of so many dancers from different tribes sharing the day. Moose's family is descended from the Apache tribe, and he also has ancestors who were Winnebago, Mojave, and Omaha. Little Man's family

Visitors watch a dancer from outside the sacred dance circle.

belongs to the Abenaki tribe. But at powwows, tribal differences melt away in friendship. All are Native Americans who share pride in their heritage and traditions. The only rivalry is friendly competition in the dance circle, and all dancers are united by the singing and the heartbeat of the drum.

Little Man is glad that non-Indian visitors are invited to come to the powwow. He wants them to experience the traditions of his people, who had lived in the Americas long before Europeans arrived. Everywhere Little Man looks as he dances by, he sees families enjoying a time of togetherness, celebrating the day.

~3~

THE POWWOW TRAIL

For most of the year, Little Man attends public school with his friends. He is called by his American name, Joel. He lives with his older brother, younger sister, and parents in a town in western Massachusetts. His parents have a gift shop filled with Native American art and crafts, and he often helps out after school and on weekends when he isn't playing school sports. All year long, the family works together to make craft items, which they sell from a booth at powwows during the summer.

As soon as the powwow season begins in the spring, Little Man and his family spend weekends traveling around the east-

24

Plains-style teepees are set up at some eastern powwow campsites.

ern states and camping at gatherings run by different tribes. They go to powwows every weekend from April through October. Many call this "traveling the powwow trail." Most powwows are within one day's drive of their home. Some powwows last only two days during a weekend; others take advantage of a holiday weekend and go on for three days. Occasionally, a well-attended powwow lasts up to five days, but that is rare.

At each gathering, the family sets up their crafts booth, and Little Man and his sister, Julia, dance in the events. At powwows, everyone calls Little Man by his Indian name. Often, the booth is so busy with shoppers that Little Man helps sell items and answer questions about things the family has made. But there is always time to do other things. He visits friends, dances in the circle, trades for interesting crafts, and plays games that last far into the night. There is no early bedtime at a powwow. Late each night he crawls into the tent, exhausted and happy.

Everyone in Little Man's family is artistic. His mother weaves **dream catchers** using hoops of grapevine webbed with fiber. They hang from the top of the booth, their feather decorations blowing in the breeze. A Chippewa (Ojibwa) story says that when a dream catcher is placed over your bed, good dreams pass through the webbing,

An unusual dream catcher design

Little Man and his sister Julia travel the powwow trail all summer with their mother and father.

but bad dreams are caught until daylight, when they lose their power and fade away. Little Man tries to remember his dreams. Some of his friends dream their Indian names. Others dream about the colors or designs to use in their regalia or face paint.

Little Man's older brother, Jim, airbrushes shirts and jackets with Native American designs. His mother also beads necklaces and weaves bracelets with beads and colored string. They dangle from wooden display stands on the counter of the booth. His father carves and builds wooden marionettes. They stand on the counter, their faces decorated with paint and their clothing sewn in traditional styles. At one end, candles which Little Man has helped make, are piled in baskets. To make the candles, they dye hot wax and scent it with sage, sweet grass, or cranberries. Then they pour each batch of candle wax carefully into molds, insert a wick, and let them harden. Little Man smells the candles wherever he stands in the booth. Powwows are traditionally a time of gift giving, and Little Man often gives one to a new friend.

Moose lives in Connecticut and travels with his family to weekend powwows. Nearly everyone in Moose's family dances. His mother is often chosen to lead the procession as head dancer for Women's Traditional Dance. It is a great honor.

The boys make a new friend this weekend. Diami, whose name means Eagle, is Mohegan and Cherokee. Although he lives in Arizona, he is traveling the Eastern powwow circuit with his grandmother and cousin. His cousin is a Native American flute player and singer. He plays at powwows and sells tapes of his music.

Diami prefers to watch the dancing. He dresses in street clothes and helps the singers set up the powwow drums before the dancing begins. At some powwows, there are many different drum groups, and occasionally they compete with each other for the best singing.

Diami tells his friends that powwows in the Plains states and the Southwest often begin with a

huge parade, with decorated cars and trucks and many floats. There are always horses at those gatherings, and they are usually painted with designs and adorned with blankets and sometimes with feathers. At some of these powwows, there is a rodeo, as well. Eastern powwows feature dancing, and there are rarely any horses or other events.

Moose and Little Man became friends at a powwow when they were ten years old.

DRUM GROUPS

No powwow could go on without the drumming and singing that accompanies the dancers. The drum, or host drum, as the musical group is called, is the heartbeat of the gathering and gives the dancers their energy. A drum usually is all men, although women and young people can also learn the songs and participate. There is one lead singer, who is also a drummer, and at least four additional members.

Drums are set up under a shaded arbor near the entrance to the dance circle. There is a large rawhide covered drum, sometimes painted with designs. It sits on a wooden stand, and drummers strike the beat with padded sticks. Some powwows have just one drum, but large powwows often have several set up around the inside of the dance circle. Some names of drum groups on the Eastern powwow circuit are Mystic River, Red Hawk, and Eagle Heart.

Singers usually present traditional songs from various tribes, but often new songs are also introduced. At some Eastern gatherings, the drums sing mainly Algonquian songs. Some songs preserve the language of a tribe or group, but others use vocables (repeated sounds) to keep the melody and the beat.

~4~
TIME
TO
DANCE!

After the opening procession, the three boys settle down on a hay bale to watch the adult dancing. Low stools and hay bales are placed around the inside of the circle so dancers can rest. Dancing uses a lot of energy, even on a cool day!

"It's a good thing there are no backs on these seats," Moose says, "or the feathers on my bustle would get crushed. Either that, or I wouldn't be able to sit down at all!"

Cassie squeezes onto the hay bale, too. She lifts her slim dress nearly to her waist, and the boys laugh when they see that she is wearing shorts underneath.

"Well, I can't sit on these jingles," she says.

Women traditional dancers carry shawls folded over their arms.

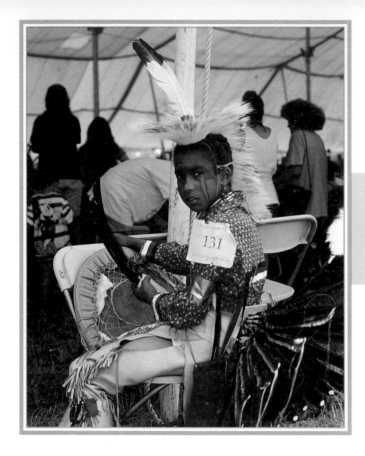

A traditional dancer sits backwards on his chair so he won't crush his delicate feather bustle.

The announcer calls for Women's Traditional to begin. The participants stand proudly, each with a bright fringed shawl folded over one arm. Their printed competition numbers are pinned on their shawls. Some are dressed in white or buff-colored buckskin dresses. Others wear bright cloth dresses. On most outfits, long fringes hang from sleeves and hems. Tall, beaded moccasins rise toward their knees.

The women dancers have fixed their hair in one or two long braids, and some have added a wispy feather plume. Many wear long deer-bone aprons, called a hairpipe breastplates, which cover the front of their dresses. Fancy beadwork traces colorful designs on sleeves, hems, yokes, belts, and moccasins.

When the stately Women's Traditional ends, the announcer calls for Girls' Jingle Dress dancing. Cassie jumps up and smooths her dress. Moose doesn't say anything as Cassie walks off, but Little Man can tell by his smile that he is proud of his sister.

The circle fills with young women in the special dresses, and the singers begin a lively song. Moose and his friends agree that Cassie is one of the best dancers. She moves with high, energetic steps. Her feet are so light as she touches the ground that she seems to fly like a bird. The pleasant sound of the jingles fills the arena.

"Get ready, Traditional Boys!" shouts the announcer. "It's almost time for the **Sneak Up!**" This is Little Man's favorite. He jumps up from the hay bale, ready to dance. He picks up his fan, made from feathers of a red-tail hawk, and makes sure his head roach is tight.

"Where did you get this fan?" Diami asks. Little Man explains that he and his father made almost all his regalia. Each item takes a great deal of time and effort. They have tied every porcupine hair on his roach with five deer hairs before

ORIGINS OF THE JINGLE DRESS

Like most dances that are performed today, there are different stories about how the Jingle Dress Dance began. Linda Wade Koslowski of the Mille Lacs band of Chippewa (Ojibwa) tells that long ago, a father prayed to the Great Spirit to cure his daughter, who was very sick. One night, the Sacred Spirits came to him in a dream. They showed him a special dress and told him how it was to be made. They revealed special songs and dance moves. The women of the village helped sew the dress according to his vision. They sewed seven rows of tin cones, fashioned from tobacco can lids, on the slim dress. When the daughter danced to the new songs in the sacred jingle dress, she was cured.

The jingle dress was worn for many years by Chippewa women dancers, and it was common among the Lakota, as well. The dance spread to many Plains tribes. At today's powwows, jingle dresses are made of colorful patterned cloth, and rows and rows of jingles are attached all along the slim dress. Jingle Dress dancers keep their hands close to their bodies as they perform the intricate, high steps of the dance. The metal cones jingle in time to the beat of the drum.

Regalia is made with much care and tradition.

attaching them to the headpiece. He has painted a black bear on his copper neck piece, called a **gorget**. Fringed buckskin leggings, a fabric breechcloth with long trailers, and a breastplate completes his outfit. Sometimes, he adds a cloth shirt with flowing ribbons to his regalia.

Little Man shows Diami a few special pieces he has added to his regalia. A friend has made a leather case to hold Little Man's knife, which is carved from a fox jaw. Diami carefully rubs his finger across the fox teeth that remain on its edge. Just above each of Little Man's knees, a string of deer toes hangs loosely.

"These were made from dried deer toes," Little Man tells his friend. When strung together in clusters, they make a clacking rattle that adds to the sounds of the dancing.

As the Girls' Jingle Dress dancing ends, Little Man walks to the opening. He loves the Sneak Up Dance because it makes him feel like a traditional warrior. He takes a place in the dance circle and grips his fan and **coup stick**, a smooth stick with a pheasant's claw attached to the end. Whenever he dances, he is careful to aim the sharp claw tip toward the ground, away from other dancers. An elder told him that in earlier times, many believed that if a warrior touched his defeated enemy with his coup stick, it destroyed the victim's bravery.

If a warrior could come close enough to touch his enemy and escape without injuring him, that warrior would be honored by the tribe for his skill and courage.

In the Sneak Up, each dancer imitates a warrior scout tracking an enemy, or a hunter tracking an animal. Little Man balances on one knee as the drummers beat a fast tempo that sounds like thunder. He shades his eyes with his feather fan and turns his head left and right, as if looking off into the distance. With his coup stick, he points to imaginary tracks on the ground and shakes one leg in time to the drum.

The drumming changes to a moderate beat. Little Man and the other young dancers move forward in a fast tap step. Like true warriors, they always advance, never retreat. They bend low, as if searching the ground for tracks, and turn their heads and bodies slightly in the direction of each new step. Little Man's feather bustle sways with his steps.

Little Man listens carefully to the singing and the drum. A louder, deeper pattern of words means the song is about to end. He must start and end with the first and last beats. The deer toe rattles must fall silent as he stops. Little Man counts beats in his head and stands still on the very last drumbeat.

◄ In the Sneak Up Dance, Little Man holds his coup stick with a pheasant's claw attached to one end.

"Good dancing," says Moose, when Little Man rejoins his friends. "You get better all the time."

"I listen to the drum along with my heartbeat," Little Man explains, "and my feet just dance!"

Moose heads off to the circle for the Junior Boys' Traditional Dance. All the dancers wear elaborate regalia and paint their faces. Different colors have special meanings, and dancers choose their face paint to reflect their personal thoughts.

At one powwow, Little Man talked to a woman who made body paint from different materials. She told him that traditionally, colored paints were made from boiled fruits and vegetables, such as beets, corn, grass, and blueberries. They also used certain bugs, flowers, and tree bark. The resulting colors were mixed with fats or oils so they could be applied to the skin. She and other young women had learned to make these paints in the old way.

Little Man rarely wears face paint, but today Moose has red and yellow stripes across his nose and cheeks. Moose is the only one who knows the personal meaning of his design. Perhaps he has dreamed it. Little Man won't ask his friend to tell him.

The dance steps are fast, and the drumming quick. As the song draws to a close, the notes become lower in pitch, and the drum booms faster and louder. Moose stomps one foot and freezes on the last beat. All of the dancers hold still for a moment before they relax and leave the dance circle.

"Now let's eat!" Diami announces. "I'm starving!"

COLORS FROM THE EARTH

Many dancers use body paint or face paint. Traditionally, some warriors painted their bodies to look fierce to their enemies, but paint was mostly used for ceremonial or religious reasons, or as a personal expression. Ceremonial body paint was often worn to insure abundant rain and a good harvest, a successful hunt, or the continued increase in the tribe's population.

Different colors can symbolize several things. Red can represent life, as well as the blood that makes life possible. It can signify war, power, and success. Yellow represents the sun, happiness, bravery, or the dawn of each new day. Green is for plants, rain, and the growing season of summer. Brown reflects the soil and Mother Earth. White is the color of peace, and also of winter, snow, death, and the Spirit World. Blue represents the sacred sky, water, moon, or clouds. It can also signify sadness or defeat.

Bright feathers fly during a Young Men's Fancy Dance competition.

~5~

WATCHING
TEACHES
DANCING

DIAMI LEADS THE WAY to the fry bread stand, and the boys bring back a snack to eat while they watch the adult dancing. Little Man likes the regalia of the Fancy Dancers, with fringed clothes and strings of leg bells. They always wear two feather bustles—a large traditional back bustle and a smaller neck bustle. They also have small bustles attached to their upper arms. They carry turtle-shell shields, feather fans, or decorated dance sticks. Fancy Dancers rarely wear face paint, but their bright, colorful clothing and swirling, high-step dancing is thrilling.

Moose and Little Man learn new steps and pick up pointers to improve their own dancing as they watch. At one powwow, Little

Man held a dancer's belongings while he competed. To thank him, the dancer showed Little Man a special step.

There is no formal training for Native American dances, and Little Man is glad that he doesn't have to take lessons to learn. He thinks it is better to learn by watching and then dance what you feel. Children start imitating their parents and elders as soon as they are old enough to walk. Little Man's younger sister, Julia, who is six years old, began by dancing the Traditional Women's steps in the Tiny Tots category. Now she is a Jingle Dress dancer in the Girls' Division. Although she is among the youngest dancers in the group, she dances well and tries new steps.

Little Man feels his dancing is improving because when the drumming begins, his body moves to its rhythm automatically. He doesn't have to think of his steps, but simply feels his movements are part of the song. Sometimes he practices at home by listening to tapes of traditional songs. Like all the dancers who compete for prizes, Little Man doesn't reveal all his moves in the opening procession. He saves his fanciest steps for the competition.

At many powwows, there are special exhibition dances. At this one, Aztec dancers from

Julia holds her feather fan and practices a few steps before heading to the dance circle. ➤

Mexico City perform an exciting Eagle Dance and a traditional Fire Dance. Another dancer performs a skillful **Hoop Dance**. He spreads large hoops on the ground, and as the singing and drumming begins, he flips them onto his ankles, legs, arms, and body. Then he manipulates them into shapes—an eagle with wings spread wide, a fluttering butterfly, and the round circle of Earth. With each new design, spectators whistle and cheer.

"Okay, dancers, take a break!" calls the announcer. "The cooks stirring buffalo stew have offered to feed the singers to thank them for their good music. Let's give the drum a little rest. Meanwhile, we've got some great storytelling coming up, so all of you sitting outside the circle, you've got a treat in store!"

Cassie and the boys head back to their campsites for their own lunch. Little Man wants to help at the booth and doesn't stay to listen to the storyteller who entertains the crowd with traditional Native American tales. He will hear the elders tell many stories as they sit around the campfires at night, after the spectators have gone home.

Many visitors browse at the crafts stands until dancing begins again. Little Man stays at the booth to help his family while people mill around and buy their handmade items. Nearby, a Navajo

◀ **Adriana, a member of the Tlacopan Aztec Dancers of Mexico City**

47

POWWOW MANNERS

When you go to a powwow remember that you are a guest. You will be a welcome visitor if you remember to follow the powwow ways.

1. Always listen to the speaker. The announcer will tell you which event is about to take place and will say whether or not photographs are allowed.

2. Take off your hat when the flags are carried into the circle during the grand entry. Keep your hat off to honor the veterans who will enter the circle next.

3. Save your picture-taking for the intertribal dances that take place after the opening ceremonies. If you would like to take a photograph of a dancer outside the circle, ask permission first.

4. Watch the dancers from outside the sacred dance circle. Visitors should not enter the circle unless they are invited by the announcer to take part.

5. If you are invited to dance, join in! Always enter the circle from the opening at the east end.

6. Dancers' regalia is delicate. You can admire a dancer's outfit, and ask questions about it, but don't touch any items unless they are offered to you.

7. Drums are usually set under a covered arbor. This is a sacred place, and visitors should not enter the drum area. Even when singers take a break, drums should be admired from a respectful distance. Tape-recording of drum music is not permitted without permission.

8. Respect the dance circle and Mother Earth by picking up all litter.

9. Take home lots of good feelings!

sells his mother's woven rugs. Other vendors offer silver and turquoise jewelry. There is pottery in traditional styles of different tribes. Some stands have materials to make new regalia, such as soft animal skins, feathers, bone beads, and porcupine quills. A few craftspeople offer dresses, vests, breastplates, head roaches, and artistic bustles.

The afternoon events begin with a performance by Diami's cousin. Moose and Little Man join their friend to listen to the new variations of Native American music Diami's cousin has composed. The sounds of his flute drift across the dance circle, and Little Man feels its reedy melody. Usually, the drummers proudly sing ancient songs that have been sung for hundreds of years, but new songs are welcome. Sometimes they become part of accepted traditional music as dancers and singers become familiar with them. Little Man wonders if he will see dancers stepping to the new song before too long.

Moose and Little Man are rested and ready to dance again. When the announcer invites everyone to join together in a Round Dance, one of the social dances, Cassie joins them. Moose pulls Diami from the hay bale.

"No more sitting," he scolds. "Everyone dances this one." Diami holds back at first but is soon

caught up in the spirit of the day and dances along with his friends.

The announcer invites all visitors to partici-pate. Everyone joins hands and sidesteps togeth-er to the beat of the drum. Little Man hears the laughter and feels the spirit of unity that travels through the clasped hands. It is the true spirit of the powwow. After the spectators return to their seats, the dancing continues. All afternoon, into the evening, the beat of the drum thunders through the air.

The members of the host drum are tired after a day under the hot summer sun. The dancers are getting tired, too. The announcer decides to end the festivities with a playful **Switch Dance**. For this event, women put on some of the men's regalia and do a spirited Traditional Dance. Men borrow the women's shawls and swing them in the Fancy Shawl Dance.

Cassie smiles shyly as Moose fastens his large feather bustle over her jingle dress and hands her his feather fan. The girls and women do their best to imitate the men's dance steps. There is much friendly teasing. Then the men drape fringed shawls over their regalia and spread their arms in a fast version of the women's dance. Everyone laughs, and the crowd applauds the dancers and the host drum.

Moose, Cassie, and Little Man join all the dancers for the closing ceremonies. The color guard returns and leads them around the circle. They retire the flags and the drum as they wind their way out through the opening in the circle.

~6~

CLAMBAKES & FIREBALLS IN THE NIGHT

THE DANCING IS OVER, but Little Man and his friends still have enough energy for the evening activities. At this powwow, members of the tribe prepare a traditional Wampanoag clambake. White-hot stones hiss as the men cover them with wet, salty seaweed. They set bundles of clams, lobsters, mussels, and sweet corn on top of the stones and watch as the food cooks in the hot steam.

Before the brown lobsters turn red, and the shellfish open to reveal their tender meat, the boys head back to their families. Little Man helps pack away everything in the booth and do some errands around camp for his parents.

As the sun falls lower in the sky, the flags are retired in a closing ceremony.

Like the other dancers, he carefully stores his regalia and changes into jeans and a T-shirt.

After the clambake feast, the sun sets behind campers and tents, and darkness falls. Tonight the host tribe will play the Wampanoag fireball game. Little Man's father says that in earlier times, the game was played to provide medicine for the sick. This meant that the game was held to ask the Creator to help cure anyone in the tribe who was ill. One of the Wampanoag men says the game was originally played on the beach at the ocean's edge, with the goalposts as far as a mile apart. Pilgrim settlers saw the game and wrote about it in their journals.

Little Man and Moose wish they were old enough to play, but the game is so fast and dangerous that only teenage and adult men are allowed to participate. Little Man, Moose, and Diami climb a tree at the edge of the field for a good view.

"Here comes the torch," Moose says, and a runner lights the tops of two goalposts placed at each end of the dark field. The burning goalposts will be the only source of light throughout the game, so the players can guide the ball toward them.

The tightly wrapped cloth ball is about the size of a soccer ball. A runner drops it between two teams at the center of the playing field. Then he touches it with his torch and stands back. Immediately, the game begins. Players kick the flaming ball toward the goalposts. Some of them run swiftly through the darkness and kick the fireball with bare feet.

"Pick it up! Pick it up!" chants the crowd, and a brave player picks up the blazing ball in his hands and hurls it toward the burning goalposts. Little Man strains to watch the silhouettes of the players running across the dark field.

No one counts how many times the ball passes into the goal. Neither team wins or loses. Instead, they play for the thrill of the game. After about a half hour of spirited play, the ball burns down, leaving bits and pieces of cloth smoldering into embers on the damp grass. The game is over. The boys climb down from their perch and file back to the campground with the rest of the crowd. Even they are tired now.

Tomorrow will be the last day of the powwow, a final day of drumming, dancing, and eating fry bread. Little Man and his friends often exchange farewell gifts. And there will be talk about the next big gathering.

Little Man crawls into his sleeping bag. His mother has hung a dream catcher from the wall of the tent, and it sways in the evening breeze. He closes his eyes to sleep.

◄ **The spirit of the day spans all ages. Keon, a two-year-old Wampanoag (top) and Grandfather Oak, a ninety-three-year-old Huron elder (bottom), both dance at the powwow.**

Tomorrow will be a good day to dance.

POWWOW TERMS

breastplate ~ a rectangular chest covering, often made of bone beads

breechcloth ~ a loincloth worn by Native American men, usually made of leather or cloth, and often embroidered in decorative patterns

coup stick ~ a warrior's stick, used to touch an enemy as an act of bravery

deer toes ~ dried dewclaws, taken from the hoof of a deer. These are sometimes strung together and worn as leg rattles.

dream catcher ~ a hoop in various sizes, webbed across the center

Fancy Dance ~ a fast war dance for men in which they wear two feather bustles

Fancy Shawl Dance ~ a high-stepping, quick women's dance in which the dancers open their shawls in outstretched arms

feather bustle ~ a circle of feathers worn at the back, or on the back of the neck

fry bread ~ thick fried dough usually topped with sugar

gorget ~ a protective or decorative metal piece worn over the throat

Grass Dance ~ a men's dance, originating with the Plains tribes, in which dancers wear fringed outfits

hairpipe tubes ~ long beads, usually made of animal bone, used to make men's breastplates and women's aprons

Hoop Dance ~ a dance, thought to originate with the Chippewa (Ojibwa), in which the dancer manipulates various hoops into different patterns without losing the rhythm of the dance steps

host drum ~ a group of singers and drummers seated around a large drum who make the music for the dancers. Also sometimes called simply, "the drum."

Jingle Dress Dance ~ a women's dance in which the dancers wear a dress covered with rows of tin cones that jingle as they move

medicine wheel ~ a round hoop of wood or metal, representing the earth, with a horizontal and vertical piece intersecting through the middle, usually painted with red, white, black, and yellow, to represent the four directions. An eagle feather often hangs from the center.

Men's Traditional Dance ~ a slow war dance

regalia ~ Native American clothing and items worn or carried during traditional events

roach ~ a stiff headpiece, usually made of porcupine hairs, worn by men

Sneak Up Dance ~ a traditional men's dance in which the dancer imitates a hunter or warrior tracking an animal or an enemy

Switch Dance ~ a humorous event in which men and women trade regalia and perform each other's traditional dances

vocables ~ repeated sounds that keep the melody and beat during dancing

Women's Traditional Dance ~ a slow, stately dance in which women usually carry a folded shawl over one arm

TO FIND OUT MORE

BOOKS

Ancona, George. *Powwow*. San Diego: Harcourt Brace Jovanovich, 1993.

Hirschfelder, Arlene. *Native American Almanac*. Prentice-Hall, 1993.

Hoxie, Frederick. *Encyclopedia of North American Indians*. Boston: Houghton Mifflin, 1996.

Roberts, Chris. *Powwow Country*. Montana: American and World Geographic Publishing, 1992.

Siegel, Beatrice. *Indians of the Northeast Woodlands*. New York: Walker, 1992.

ORGANIZATIONS AND ONLINE SITES

A Guide to the Great Sioux Nation
http://www.state.sd.us/state/executive/tourism/sioux/sioux.htm

This site offers an overview of South Dakota's tribes. A specific section on powwows discusses manners, displays a collection of photos, and lists a full schedule of powwows being held in South Dakota.

The Lenni Lenape Historical Society and Museum of Indian Culture
2825 Fish Hatchery Road
Allentown, PA 18103
(610) 797-2121
http://www.lenape.org/

In addition to describing this fascinating museum, this website has a helpful calendar of powwows and other events held all over the United States and Canada.

The Native American Artists' Home Page
http://www.artnatam.com/

This website features an online exhibit with a display of artwork from a variety of Native American artists.

National Museum of the American Indian
The George Gustav Heye Center
Alexander Hamilton U. S. Custom House
One Bowling Green
New York, NY 10004
(212) 668-6624
http://www.si.edu/nmai/

The National Museum of the American Indian contains exciting collections of artifacts, artwork, films, and books. At their website, read about the museum's exhibits and abundant resources.

INDEX

ABOUT THE AUTHOR

JACQUELINE DEMBAR GREENE attended her first powwow in Mashpee, Massachusetts, where she met Little Man, Moose, and their families. Both boys explained their regalia and their dancing and introduced her to friends and family on the pow-wow circuit who shared their traditions. Mrs. Greene has since attended numerous eastern states pow-wows and completed research and interviews on dances, music, and Native American culture. She has also sampled her fair share of fry bread! Her photographs of dancers, their individual regalia, and pow-wow events help her share the excitement and friendship that flows through the gatherings. Mrs. Greene's husband, Malcolm, accompanied her to powwows, helping with photographic equipment and sharing in the spirit of the events.

A former journalist, Mrs. Greene is an award-winning author of numerous picture books, nonfiction, and novels for young readers. Her historical novels, *Out of Many Waters* and *One Foot Ashore*, were both named Sydney Taylor Honor Books. She has written other books in the Indians of the Americas First Books series, including *The Maya*, *The Chippewa*, and *The Tohono O'odham*.